IDEAS FOR STORAGE

IDEAS PARA GUARDAR

IDÉES DE RANGEMENT

IDEEN ZUM AUFBEWAHREN

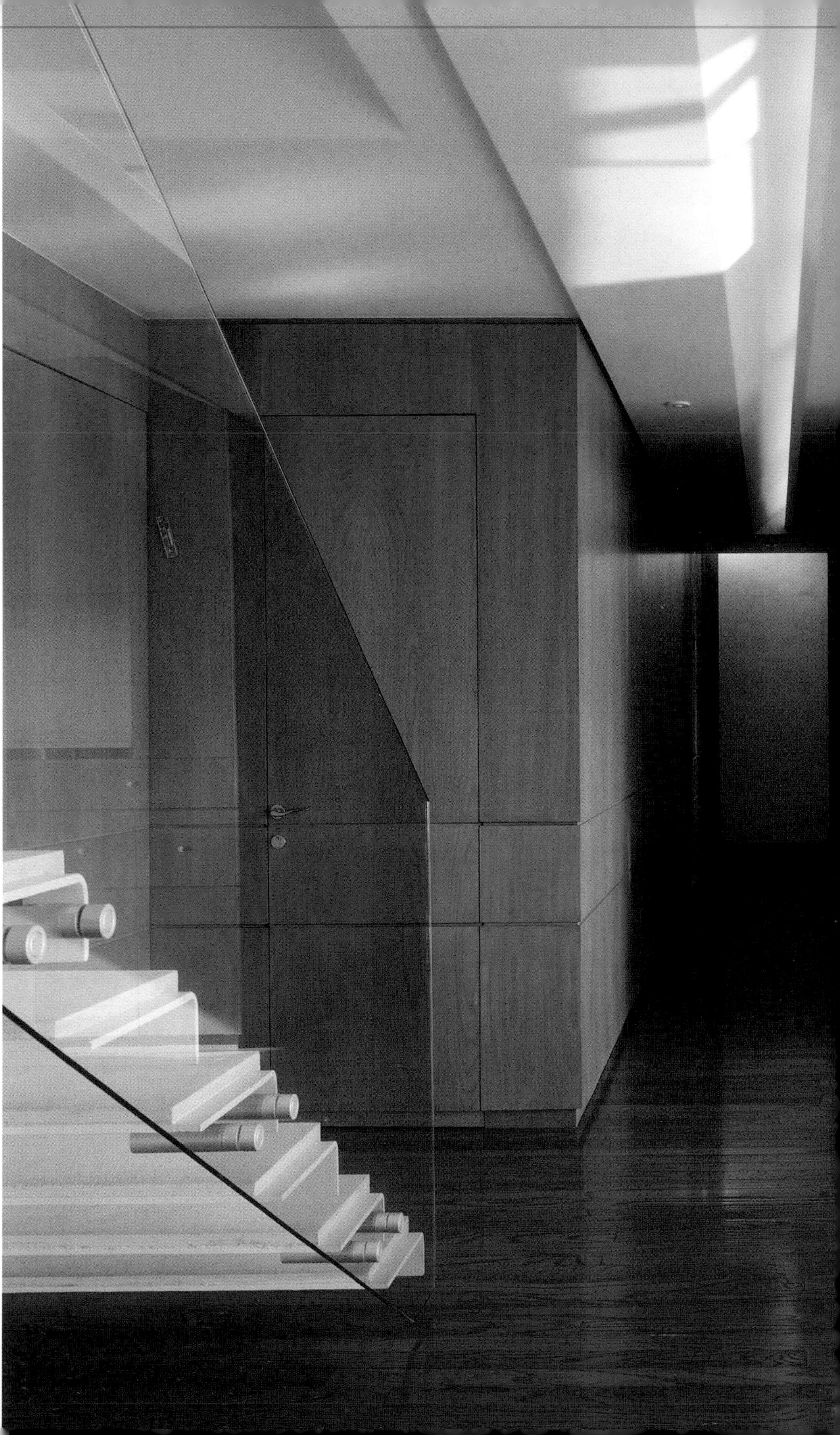

AUTHORS
Fernando de Haro & Omar Fuentes

EDITORIAL DESIGN & PRODUCTION
AM Editores S.A. de C.V.

PROJECT MANAGERS
Valeria Degregorio Vega
Tzacil Cervantes Ortega

COORDINATION
Edali Núñez Daniel
Martha Guerrero Martel

COPYWRITERS
Abraham Orozco
Roxana Villalobos

ENGLISH TRANSLATION
Louis Loizides

FRENCH TRANSLATION
Wordgate Translations

GERMAN TRANSLATION
Heike Ruttkowski

EDITORES

PUBLISHERS

100+ TIPS · IDEAS
ideas for storage . ideas para guardar
idées de rangement . ideen zum aufbewahren

© 2009, Fernando de Haro & Omar Fuentes
AM Editores S.A. de C.V.
Paseo de Tamarindos 400 B, suite 102, Col. Bosques de las Lomas, C.P. 05120, México, D.F.
Tels. 52(55) 5258 0279, Fax. 52(55) 5258 0556. ame@ameditores.com **www.ameditores.com**

ISBN 13: 978-607-437-022-5

Printed in China.

INTRODUCTION
INTRODUCCIÓN
INTRODUCTION
EINLEITUNG

The supreme practicality of ideas for storing things provides plenty of food for thought and excellent solutions for the architects, interior designers and occupants of any home. The aim is to provide tips and pointers to help families store that entire universe of objects and articles they invariably possess, including clothing, bed linen, tablecloths and napkins, day to day utensils, books, ornaments, works of art, family mementoes and anything else that needs to be put away, hidden or displayed, as the case may be, in the most stylish and comfortable manner possible.

Choosing where to keep these things is important, as are the qualities of the item of furniture to be used, such as its design, materials and finish. It can be placed by the entrance to the house or in the main hall, dining room, kitchen, bathroom, bedroom, changing room or bar. It can be made of wood, glass, a combination of the two, or metal and decorative stone, with or without doors and panels, drawers and shelves, or it can be a small item of furniture for which a special corner has been set aside or a large structure that takes up a whole wall or even several. It can also stretch from the floor to the ceiling, be double height, as well as have alcoves or stairs for reaching the top. This book offers a huge array of useful and physically appealing ideas, limited only by the imagination and the size of the area.

La función eminentemente práctica de las ideas para guardar ofrece un terreno fértil para la imaginación del arquitecto, del interiorista y de los moradores de una casa que siempre podrán encontrar una manera satisfactoria de resolverla. Su misión es la de almacenar ese universo de objetos y artículos de todo tipo que las familias poseen: ropa, blancos, mantelería, utensilios para las actividades diarias, libros, objetos decorativos, obras de arte, recuerdos familiares y muchos más que deben guardarse, ocultarse o exhibirse, según el caso, con el mejor gusto y la mayor comodidad posibles.

La elección del sitio donde debe ubicarse es importante, pero también lo son las cualidades del mueble, su diseño, los materiales, el acabado. Puede instalarse en el recibidor o presidir la sala principal; en el comedor o en la cocina; el cuarto de baño, la recámara, el vestidor o el bar de la casa. De madera, de cristal o una combinación de ambos, o con metales y piedras decorativas, con entrepaños, con puertas o sin ellas, con cajoneras, con anaqueles, muebles pequeños en rincones selectos o grandes estructuras que cubren un muro, o varios. De piso a techo, de doble altura, con galerías, con escaleras para dominar su altura. Un sinfín de ideas que sólo tienen como límite la imaginación y las dimensiones del espacio, pero siempre útiles y, preferentemente, estéticos.

Les idées de rangement dont la fonction est éminemment pratique constituent un terrain fertile pour l'imagination de l'architecte, du décorateur d'intérieur ou des résidents qui trouveront toujours un moyen de ranger un ensemble d'objets et d'articles communs à toute maison : vêtements, linge de toilette et de table, ustensiles à usage quotidien, livres, objets décoratifs, œuvres d'art, souvenirs familiaux et beaucoup d'autres choses encore que l'on doit, selon les cas, ranger, dissimuler ou exhiber tout en veillant à l'esthétique et au côté pratique des solutions adoptées.

Où placer un meuble de rangement est très important mais l'esthétique de ce dernier (le design, les matériaux utilisés, les finitions) l'est tout autant. On peut placer un tel meuble dans une entrée ou bien en vue dans la pièce principale, dans une salle à manger, une cuisine, une salle de bain, une chambre, un dressing ou un coin bar. Ce meuble peut être en bois ou en verre (ou les deux) ou être décoré avec du métal ou de la pierre. Autres options : un meuble ouvert ou fermé, avec des rayonnages, des tiroirs, des étagères, de petit format et placé dans le coin spécifique d'une pièce, de grande taille et recouvrant un ou plusieurs murs ou très haut et allant du sol au plafond. Il peut comporter deux hauteurs, avec quelques marches pour en profiter ou être traversé par un passage. Les solutions possibles sont donc presque infinies. Les seules limites imposées : notre imagination, les dimensions de l'endroit, l'utilité et, si possible, l'esthétique du meuble.

Die äusserst praktische Funktion der Ideen zum Aufbewahren bietet viele Möglichkeiten für die Kreativität des Architekten, des Innendekorateurs und der Hausbewohner, die immer eine zufriedenstellende Lösung finden können. Ihre Mission ist es, eine riesige Vielfalt an Gegenstanden und Artikeln jeder Art unterzubringen, die in jeder Familie vorhanden sind: Kleidung, Handtücher und Bettwäsche, Tischdecken, Utensilien für den täglichen Gebrauch, Bücher, Dekorationsgegenstände, Kunstwerke, Erinnerungsstücke der Familie und vieles mehr, was aufbewahrt, verborgen oder ausgestellt werden soll, je nachdem was gewünscht wird, und dies mit dem besten Geschmack und der grösstmöglichen Bequemlichkeit. Die Wahl des Ortes, an dem das Möbel aufgestellt werden soll, ist wichtig. Ebenso wichtig sind aber auch das Design, die Materialien und die Oberflächenbehandlung. Es kann im Eingangsbereich oder im Wohnzimmer aufgestellt werden, im Esszimmer oder in der Küche, im Badezimmer, Schlafzimmer, im Ankleideraum oder in der Hausbar. Es kann aus Holz oder Glas oder aus einer Kombination beider Materialien gefertigt werden, oder mit Metallen und dekorativen Steinen, mit Regalbrettern, mit oder ohne Türen, mit Schubladen oder mit Einteilungen. Es kann sich um kleine Möbel handeln, die in Ecken angebracht werden oder um grosse Strukturen, die eine ganze Wand oder mehrere Wände bedecken. Vom Boden bis zur Decke, doppelte Deckenhöhe, mit Galerien oder mit Treppen, zum Erreichen der gesamten Höhe. Es ist eine endlose Vielfalt an Ideen vorhanden, die lediglich durch die Kreativität und die Ausmasse des Raumes begrenzt sind. Diese Möbel sind aber immer nützlich und vorzugsweise auch ästhetisch.

CLOSETS

CLÓSETS

DRESSING

SCHRÄNKE

The architectural conception for the inside of the home usually includes a closet, whose design and materials must blend in well with the overall style of the residence. Its design should be discrete and simple to make sure it does not overshadow the details and finishes in the bedroom or bathroom. Furthermore, even though its role is primarily a functional one, this should not prevent its physical appearance from making an esthetic contribution to the rest of the decoration or even actually defining the decorative style.

The most commonly used material, albeit not the only one, is wood with different treatments, depending on where it is used, which could be the bedroom, dressing room or bathroom.

The space for keeping towels in, along with bathroom items, toilet paper and other objects, is usually an item of furniture placed in the washbasin area to cover the piping. But there are also many other options, such as floor to ceiling closets finished with damp- and temperature-resistant materials, wood, glass, acrylic or others. They may even be built in the form of a dressing room. The design will be determined by user needs, the size of the room and the style of the house.

La disposición del clóset se incluye habitualmente en el concepto arquitectónico de los interiores en virtud de que su diseño y los materiales con que está fabricado deben armonizar con el estilo general de la casa. Su diseño suele ser discreto y sobrio a fin de no eclipsar los detalles y acabados del mobiliario del dormitorio o el cuarto de baño y aunque su función es eminentemente práctica, esa circunstancia no excluye la posibilidad de que su apariencia contribuya estéticamente con el resto de la decoración e incluso posea una personalidad propia.

El espacio para guardar toallas, artículos de tocador, papel higiénico y otros objetos se suele resolver con un mueble que generalmente se construye en el área de lavabos, cubriendo las tuberías. Existen muchas otras opciones como muebles de piso a techo, terminados con materiales resistentes a la humedad y a los cambios de temperatura, madera, cristal, acrílicos, entre otros e incluso puede construirse como un vestidor. La calidad de los diseños varía de acuerdo con las necesidades de los usuarios, las dimensiones del espacio y el estilo de la casa.

La conception d'une demeure prend généralement en compte la présence d'un dressing afin d'intégrer son design ainsi que les matériaux utilisés pour sa fabrication à l'harmonie générale de la maison. Son design doit donc donc rester discret et sobre pour ne pas masquer les détails et les finitions du mobilier environnant dans une chambre ou une salle de bain. Toutefois, bien que sa fonction primaire soit éminemment pratique, son apport esthétique au reste de la décoration n'est pas à négliger et il peut même parfois apporter une touche d'originalité à l'ensemble. Serviettes, articles de toilettes, papier hygiénique et autres objets sauront trouver leur place dans un meuble généralement proche des lavabos et couvrant la tuyauterie. Il existe de nombreuses possibilités comme les meubles utilisant toute la hauteur de plafond, avec des finitions à base de matériaux résistants à l'humidité et aux changements de températures : bois, verre, acrylique, entre autres. On peut même envisager d'en faire un placard à vêtements. Son design sera déterminé par l'usage que les propriétaires veulent en faire, les dimensions de l'espace et le style de la maison.

Der Schrank wird normalerweise in das architektonische Konzept im Innenbereich mit einbezogen, da dessen Design und die Materialien, aus denen er hergestellt wird, mit dem allgemeinen Stil des Hauses harmonieren müssen. Das Design ist für gewöhnlich schlicht und einfach, damit die Aufmerksamkeit nicht von den Details und der Beschaffenheit der Möbel des Schlafzimmers oder des Badezimmers abgelenkt wird. Und obwohl die Funktion eines Schrankes besonders praktisch sein sollte, heisst dies nicht, dass er nicht gleichzeitig auch auf ästhetische Weise zu der restlichen Dekoration beitragen kann und sogar eine eigene Persönlichkeit besitzt. Das Material, das am häufigsten verwendet wird -obwohl natürlich auch anderen Materialien denkbar sind- ist Holz mit unterschiedlicher Oberflächenbehandlung, je nach dem Ort, an dem sich der Schrank befindet, wie Schlafzimmer, Ankleideraum oder Badezimmer. Der Bereich zum Aufbewahren von Handtüchern, Toilettenartikeln, Toilettenpapier und anderen Gegenständen ist meist ein Schrank, der unterhalb des Waschbeckens angebracht wird, um gleichzeitig die Rohre zu verdecken. Es gibt aber auch andere Möglichkeiten, wie Schränke vom Boden bis zur Decke, die aus Materialien gefertigt sind, die widerstandsfähig gegen Feuchtigkeit und Temperaturänderungen sind, wie Holz, Glas, Acryl usw. Die Möbel können sogar so angebracht werden, dass sie die Funktion eines Ankleideraumes übernehmen. Die Qualität des Designs hängt von den Bedürfnissen der Bewohner, dem Ausmass des Badezimmers und dem Stil des Hauses ab.

A double-fronted
wooden wardrobe
with no doors
integrates the
dressing room into
the bedroom.

Une double
armoire ouverte en
bois incorpore le
dressing dans la
salle de bain.

Un armario de
madera, de
doble frente y sin
puertas, incorpora
el vestidor al
cuarto de baño.

Ein Kleiderschrank
aus Holz mit
doppelter Front
und ohne Türen,
verbindet den
Ankleideraum mit
dem Badezimmer.

TIPS - ASTUCES - TIPPS

- It your bathroom and changing room share the same space, try to make sure that the storage area is protected from damp.
- Si tu baño y vestidor comparten espacio procura que el área de guardado quede aislada de la húmeda.
- Si la salle de bain et le dressing occupent la même pièce, faites en sorte que l'espace réservé aux vêtements reste sec.
- Wenn das Bad und das Ankleidezimmer räumlich miteinander verbunden sind, ist darauf zu achten, dass der Bereich zum Aufbewahren nicht der Feuchtigkeit ausgesetzt ist.

TIPS - ASTUCES - TIPPS
- Privacy can be afforded to the bathroom and dressing room by using polished glass to separate them.
- Para dar privacidad al baño y al vestidor divídelos con vidrio esmerilado.
- Pour faire de la salle de bain et du dressing des endroits privés, cloisonnez-les avec des séparations en verre dépoli.
- Um die Privatsphäre von Badezimmer und Ankleideraum zu wahren, können die beiden Bereiche mit einer Wand aus geschliffenem Glas voneinander getrennt werden.

This standalone item of furniture has been designed for storing bathroom garments and items, first aid kits and other common usage objects.

El diseño del mueble peninsular permite guardar ropa de baño, artículos de tocador, botiquines, entre otros objetos de uso frecuente.

Un ilot central a été conçu pour pouvoir ranger le linge de bain, les articles de toilettes ou de pharmacie et autres objets à usage courant.

Das Design des Möbels in der Mitte des Raumes dient zum Verstauen von Handtüchern, Toilettenartikeln, Utensilien und anderen Gegenständen, die häufig gebraucht werden.

This item of storage furniture with its stylish wooden design stands as the bathroom's focal point.

El mueble para guardar, de elegante diseño en madera, es el punto focal de este baño.

L'élément-clé de cette salle de bain: la forme raffinée du meuble de rangement en bois.

Das Möbel zum Aufbewahren von Gegenständen weist ein elegantes Holzdesign auf und steht im Mittelpunkt dieses Badezimmers.

TIPS - ASTUCES - TIPPS
- A suitable combination of wood tones will make the bathroom look stylish.
- La combinación tonal de las maderas te hará lucir un baño con estilo.
- Différents tons de bois donneront un style recherché à votre salle de bain.
- Die Farbkombination des Holzes verleiht dem Badezimmer Stil.

TIPS - ASTUCES - TIPPS
• *Make the most of the closet's full width, from floor to ceiling. There are always things that need keeping.*
• *Aprovecha los espacios longitudinales del clóset de piso a techo, siempre hay cosas que guardar.*
• *Profitez de toute la longueur et de toute la hauteur de la penderie, il y a toujours de choses à ranger.*
• *Nutze die längs augerichteten Bereiche des Kleiderschrankes vom Boden bis zur Decke, denn es gibt immer etwas aufzubewahren.*

These wooden wardrobes make the most of the space afforded by the bays in this bathroom.

Los armarios de madera oscura, aprovechan el espacio de los vanos de la estructura de este baño.

Les armoires en bois sont mises en valeur grâce à la lumière qui entre dans cette salle de bain.

Die Schränke aus Holz nutzen den Bereich der Öffnungen, die in der Struktur des Badezimmers vogesehen sind.

The versatile design of this wardrobe makes it ideal for keeping all types of clothes on hangers with enough room to breathe or carefully folded in spacious drawers.

Su versátil diseño es útil para guardar toda clase de ropa, colgada en ganchos, con espacio suficiente para respirar, o cuidadosamente doblada en amplias cajoneras.

Le design multifonctionnel des meubles permet de ranger tout type de vêtements, qu'ils soient pendus à des cintres avec un espace suffisant pour qu'ils respirent ou qu'ils soient soigneusement pliés dans de larges tiroirs.

Das vielseitige Design kann zum Aufbewahren jeder Art von Kleidung genutzt werden, aufgehängt auf Kleiderbügeln mit ausreichendem Platz zum atmen oder vorsichtig zusammengelegt in grosszügigen Schubladen.

TIPS - ASTUCES - TIPPS
- Open storage areas are an appealing option, but it is a good idea to leave a section closed for delicate items of clothing.
- Las zonas de guardado abiertas son atractivas, pero dejar una parte cerrada para prendas delicadas te será útil.
- Les espaces de rangement ouverts sont esthétiques mais en fermer une partie pour les vêtements fragiles constituera toujours un plus.
- Die offenen Bereiche zum Aufbewahren sind attraktiv; es sollte aber auch ein geschlossener Bereich für empfindliche Stücke vorgesehen werden.

The closet has been designed in such a way that, when it is closed, it becomes part of the same structure as the bedroom door, covering the whole wall with wood.

El diseño del clóset permite que, al cerrarlo, forme una unidad con la puerta de acceso a la recámara que cubre con madera toda la extensión del muro.

Le design de ces placards a été pensé pour qu'une fois fermés, ils ne fassent qu'un avec celui de la porte de la chambre recouvrant ainsi de bois toute la surface du mur.

Das Design des Kleiderschrankes ist so ausgerichtet, dass er bei verschlossenen Türen eine Einheit mit der Zimmertür bildet und das gesamte Ausmass der Wand somit mit Holz bedeckt ist.

TIPS · ASTUCES · TIPPS
• The purity of white in a closet will create a sensation of cleanliness.
• Con la pureza del blanco conseguirás sensación de limpieza en un clóset.
• Grâce à la pureté du blanc vous ferez de votre dressing un espace net et propre.
• Durch die Reinheit der Farbe weiss, wird dem Kleiderschrank der Eindruck von Sauberkeit verliehen.

This white-lacquered item of furniture has enough space between shelves to make it ideal for keeping sheets and towels.

Una pieza laqueada en blanco, con un amplio espacio entre los anaqueles, es ideal para almacenar blancos.

Des étagères en blanc laqué, suffisamment espacées, sont idéales pour y ranger le linge de toilette et de maison.

Ein weiss lackiertes Stück mit viel Platz zwischen den Regalbrettern ist ideal zum Aufbewahren von Bettwäsche und Handtüchern.

TIPS - ASTUCES - TIPPS
- Wooden floors tone down the coldness of a white closet.
- La madera en el piso aminorará el efecto de frialdad de un clóset blanco.
- Un sol en bois diminuera l'effet de froid associé à un dressing blanc.
- Das Holz des Bodens verringert den Eindruck von Kälte des weissen Kleiderschrankes.

TIPS - ASTUCES - TIPPS
- *Fixed drawers are vital, but space for sliding drawers will provide an element of flexibility for your storage options.*
- *Las cajoneras fijas son esenciales, pero contar con espacio para colocar cajoneras móviles brinda flexibilidad al guardado.*
- *Un meuble avec plusieurs tiroirs est essentiel, mais pouvoir placer des boîtes de rangement vous permettra une grande flexibilité dans votre organisation.*
- *Die festen Schubladen sind wichtig, aber ein Bereich mit beweglichen Schubladen, macht das Aufbewahren flexibel.*

BOOKSHELVES

LIBREROS

BIBLIOTHÈQUES

REGALE

Bookshelves perform a permanent lead role in interior design. They are usually made of wood, open or with glass doors, and can be located in small spaces or take up the whole wall, or even the whole room, stretching from floor to ceiling or halfway up, on the mezzanine or in specially made galleries. They portray the personality of the home's residents through the colors of its coverings and bindings, and the huge range of objects they can hold.

Although the primary role of bookshelves is not decorative, their esthetic contribution is sometimes very significant and they provide a great way of covering spaces in walls, or filling in the gaps between doors and windows, or next to the chimney, or toning down a double-height room.

They can be made of fine woods with exquisite finishes, or untreated wood with a rustic finish, with veneered moldings, or fixed or movable panels, with or without doors and a broad array of designs. Behind their doors, these items of furniture can hold, in addition to books, all types of papers and documents, while its panels can house things like ornaments, photos and personal souvenirs, to mention but a few.

Los libreros son protagonistas permanentes en el diseño de interiores. Generalmente de madera, abiertos o con puertas de cristal, ubicados en espacios reducidos u ocupando todo un muro, incluso una habitación entera, de piso a techo, de mediana altura, en los entrepisos, en galerías especialmente construidas, los libreros hablan de la personalidad de los habitantes de la casa con el juego cromático de sus cubiertas y encuadernaciones, además de la inagotable variedad de objetos de todo tipo que suelen contener.

Sin que ese sea su objetivo, los libreros son elementos decorativos, a veces de un alto valor estético que ofrecen una solución para cubrir espacios en los muros, entre los claros de puertas o ventanas, a los costados de una chimenea, o bien para suavizar las dimensiones de una doble altura.

Pueden ser de maderas finas, lujosamente terminadas, de madera al natural con acabados rústicos, con molduras chapadas, de entrepaños fijos o ajustables, con puertas o sin ellas y gran variedad de diseños. Además de libros, en este tipo de muebles, tras sus puertas se guarda también todo tipo de documentos y papeles, y en los entrepaños, objetos de adorno, fotografías, recuerdos personales y un sinfín de cosas más.

Les bibliothèques sont des éléments très importants pour la décoration intérieure. Elles sont en général en bois, ouvertes ou avec des portes en verre. On les place dans des espaces réduits mais elles peuvent aussi recouvrir la moitié ou tout un mur, voire même une chambre entière du sol au plafond. Elles se trouvent au niveau des mezzanines ou dans des couloirs spécialement pensés pour les accueillir. Elles révèlent la personnalité des propriétaires à travers les couleurs et les reliures des livres qu'elles contiennent, sans oublier les multiples objets qu'ils y placent. Bien qu'elles ne soient pas pensées dans cet objectif, les bibliothèques sont des éléments décoratifs quelquefois de haute valeur parce qu'elles permettent d'habiller les murs et de combler les espaces vides entre les portes et les fenêtres, à côté des cheminées, ou bien d'atténuer l'effet d'un plafond très haut.

Les bibliothèques peuvent être en bois exotiques, avec des finitions ostentatoires, ou en bois brut peu travaillé. Elles peuvent être décorées de moulures, avoir des étagères fixes ou mobiles, être fermées par des portes ou totalement ouvertes, en fait, tout est possible. Par ailleurs, derrière ses portes, outre des livres, on peut conserver des documents et papiers importants, et sur les étagères, des objets décoratifs, des photos et autres souvenirs.

Regale spielen immer eine Hauptrolle im Bereich des Innendesigns. Normalerweise sind sie aus Holz und offen oder mit Glastüren versehen. Sie befinden sich in kleinen Bereichen oder bedecken eine gesamte Wand. Sie können sogar ein ganzes Zimmer bedecken, vom Boden bis zur Decke oder halbhoch, in Halbgeschossen oder in Galerien, die speziell zu diesem Zweck geschaffen wurden. Die Bücherregale mit den farbigen Bucheinbänden sagen etwas über die Persönlichkeit der Bewohner des Hauses aus. Ferner kann dort eine unerschöpfliche Vielfalt an Gegenständen jeder Art untergebracht werden. Ohne dass dies das eigentliche Ziel ist, haben Bücherregale auch eine dekorative Funktion, teilweise sogar mit einem grossen ästhetischen Wert. Sie können sich in Freiräumen zwischen Wänden, im Oberlicht von Türen oder Fenstern oder seitlich von offenen Kaminen befinden. Oder sie dienen zur Milderung der Ausmasse einer doppelten Deckenhöhe. Sie können aus hochwertigem Holz sein, mit einer luxuriösen Oberflächenbehandlung oder aus Naturholz mit rustikalem Finish, mit furnierten Rahmen und festen oder variablen Regalbrettern, mit Türen oder ohne und sie können eine grosse Vielfalt in Bezug auf das Design aufweisen. Ausser Büchern können in dieser Art von Möbeln hinter Türen auch Dokumente und Unterlagen aufbewahrt werden. Auf den Regalbrettern können Dekorationsgegenstände, Fotos, persönliche Erinnerungsstücke und jede sonstige Art von Gegenständen aufgestellt werden.

The marble wall's texture provides a background for mahogany-colored wooden panels with contrasting moldings on the base.

Los entrepaños de madera de color caobilla, con molduras contrastantes en la base, utilizan como fondo la textura del muro de mármol.

Les étagères en bois de couleur chêne, avec des moulures différentes à la base, sont mises en valeur par la texture du mur en marbre.

Die Regalbretter aus Mahagoniholz mit einem Rahmen in Kontrastfarbe ermöglichen den Blick auf die Textur der Marmorwand im Hintergrund.

TIPS - ASTUCES - TIPPS
• If the study is adjacent to an outdoor area, then it should have a peaceful atmosphere.
• Conviene que si la biblioteca da a un espacio exterior, éste emita tranquilidad.
• Si la bibliothèque donne sur un espace extérieur, il faut que ce dernier se caractérise par le calme.
• Wenn die Bibliothek an einen Aussenbereich angrenzt, sollte diese Ruhe vermitteln.

This classic
bookshelf provides
avant-garde
furniture with a
touch of warmth.

El librero clásico
le da calidez
al diseño
contemporáneo
del mobiliario.

Une bibliothèque
de style classique
qui rehausse la
finesse du mobilier
contemporain.

Das klassische
Regal verleiht
dem modernen
Design der Möbel
Wärme.

TIPS - ASTUCES - TIPPS
- Comfortable and ergonomic seating should always be used in the study.
- Elige siempre sillas y sillones confortables y ergonómicos para la biblioteca.
- Choisissez toujours des chaises et des fauteuils confortables et ergonomiques pour la bibliothèque.
- Die Stühle und Sessel in der Bibliothek sollten immer bequem und ergonomisch sein.

Lacquered glass doors keep the dust off these side wall bookshelves.

Las puertas de vidrio lacado preservan del polvo el contenido de estos libreros que ocupan los muros laterales.

Les portes en verre opaque protègent de la poussière l'intérieur de cette bibliothèque qui couvre les deux murs latéraux.

Die Türen aus getöntem Glas verhindern das Einstauben der Bücher, die sich an den Seitenwänden befinden.

TIPS - ASTUCES - TIPPS
- *Books can be kept in open or closed spaces, depending on how practical these options are for you.*
- *La opción de tener los libros en espacios cerrados o abiertos depende de lo funcional que lo encuentres.*
- *Placer les livres dans des espaces ouverts ou fermés dépend de vos préférences en matière de commodité.*
- *Ob die Bücher in offenen oder geschlossenen Bereichen aufbewahrt werden, hängt davon ab, wie funktionell die jeweilige Variante ist.*

This simple and tasteful dark wood bookshelf is the focal point of this eclectic and highly personal lounge.

El librero de madera oscura, sobrio y elegante, es un punto focal en este salón ecléctico y muy personal.

La bibliothèque sobre et élégante en bois foncé constitue l'élément-clé de ce salon disparate et très personnel.

Das Bücherregal aus dunklem Holz ist schlicht und elegant. Es bildet einen Blickfang in diesem eklektischen und sehr persönlichen Raum.

TIPS - ASTUCES - TIPPS
- The plethora of styles in the furniture and fittings will help you create your very own style.
- La riqueza de estilos en el mobiliario y accesorios cooperará a que generes tu propio estilo.
- La richesse des styles pour le mobilier et les accessoires est si importante qu'elle vous aidera à créer votre propre langage décoratif.
- Eine Vielfalt an Stilrichtungen der Möbel und Accessoires trägt dazu bei, einen eigenen Stil zu schaffen.

A flawless rectangle is made by the wood on the wall, offering a sharp contrast with the light tones of the floor.

La madera traza una cuadrícula perfecta sobre el muro y contrasta vivamente con la claridad del piso.

Des quadrilatères parfaits en bois habillent le mur et s'opposent vivement à la clarté du sol.

Das Holz bildet ein perfektes Raster auf der Wand und kontrastiert auf lebendige Weise mit dem hellen Fussboden.

TIPS - ASTUCES - TIPPS

- *Flexible lights to guide you along the bookshelves are a very useful option.*
- *Unas lámparas flexibles que te guíen por tu librero serán siempre muy útiles.*
- *Quelques lampes flexibles qui éclairent votre bibliothèque seront toujours utiles.*
- *Flexible Lampen, die im Bereich der Bücher Licht spenden, sind immer sehr nützlich.*

The soft tones of the bookshelf's wood blend in perfectly with the different surrounding colors.

La suave tonalidad de la madera del librero, armoniza con la paleta de color de todo el conjunto.

Les tons suaves de cette bibliothèque se fondent harmonieusement dans la gamme de couleurs déployées par l'ensemble de la pièce.

Der weiche Farbton des Holzes des Bücherregales harmoniert mit der Farbpalette des gesamten Komplexes.

TIPS - ASTUCES - TIPPS
- *It is a good idea to bear in mind your biggest books when planning your bookshelf.*
- *Cuando planees tu librero, toma en consideración el volumen con mayores dimensiones que tengas.*
- *Lorsque vous pensez à votre bibliothèque, prenez en compte les dimensions maximales de l'espace dont vous disposez.*
- *Wenn das Bücherregal geplant wird, sollten die Bücher mit dem grössten Ausmass in Betracht gezogen werden.*

TIPS - ASTUCES - TIPPS
- *Why not include a space in your study that will make reading a true pleasure?*
- *Atrévete a integrar tu biblioteca a un espacio en el que la consulta pueda resultar un placer.*
- *N'hésitez pas à placer votre bibliothèque dans un espace où ce sera un plaisir de l'utiliser.*
- *Die Bibliothek sollte in einen Bereich integriert werden, an dem das Lesen zum Vergnügen wird.*

These dark wood bookshelves play a primarily decorative role.

Ces étagères en bois foncé ont été essentiellement conçues dans un but décoratif.

La función de estas estanterías de madera oscura, es esencialmente decorativa.

Die Funktion dieser Regale aus dunklem Holz ist im Wesentlichen dekorativer Natur.

TIPS - ASTUCES - TIPPS
- *Don't overlook the classic look provided by the combination of brown leather and wood.*
- *Recuerda que la piel café y la madera crean una estupenda y clásica combinación.*
- *N'oubliez pas que l'association d'un cuir marron et du bois est tout autant classique qu'extraordinaire.*
- *Die Kombination von braunem Leder mit Holz sieht immer hervorragend und klassisch aus.*

TIPS - ASTUCES - TIPPS
- Make the most of any unused spaces, such as the underside of the staircase, to make places where you can keep things.
- Aprovecha espacios desperdiciados, como la contraparte de la escalera, para generar zonas de guardado.
- Profitez des espaces inutiles, comme la contremarche des escaliers, pour en faire des zones de rangement.
- Ungenutzte Bereiche können zum Aufbewahren genutzt werden, wie zum Beispiel die Unterseite einer Treppe.

The double height wall is completely covered by a mesh of wooden niches.

Un muro de doble altura íntegramente cubierto por un panal de nichos de madera.

Le mur de la pièce et de la mezzanine est intégralement recouvert par des cases en bois.

Die Wand mit doppelter Deckenhöhe ist komplett durch ein Möbel mit Holznischen bedeckt.

TIPS - ASTUCES - TIPPS
• A highly original option that uses space to the full is the vertical library.
• Considera la opción de tener una original biblioteca vertical que te ayude a aprovechar el espacio.
• Pensez à une bibliothèque verticale et originale afin de profiter pleinement de l'espace.
• Erwäge die Möglichkeit eine originelle vertikale Bibliothek zu schaffen, die dabei hilft, den Platz optimal zu nutzen.

TIPS - ASTUCES - TIPPS
- A good bet for reaching the upper sections of tall shelves is steps that visually combine well with this item of furniture.
- Para las partes superiores de libreros altos, considera una escalera que armonice con el mueble.
- Pour les parties supérieures des bibliothèques de haute taille, pensez à un escabeau qui s'harmonise avec le meuble.
- Für die oberen Bereiche von hohen Bücherregalen, kann eine Leiter gewählt werden, die mit dem Möbel harmoniert.

The study is dominated by a double height dark wooden bookshelf with metal handles.

Un librero de doble altura, de madera oscura con chapas metálicas, preside el salón de lectura.

Une bibliothèque en bois foncé avec des poignées en métal montant jusqu'au plafond, domine superbement ce salon de lecture.

Das Bücherregal mit doppelter Deckenhöhe aus dunklem Holz und Metallbeschlägen spielt die Hauptrolle im Lesezimmer.

The novel design of these bookshelves infuses the ambience with warmth.

La originalidad del diseño de estas librerías da un toque de calidez al ambiente.

Une bibliothèque au concept original donne de la qualité à l'espace.

Die Originalität des Designs dieser Bücherregale verleiht der Atmosphäre einen warmen Touch.

TIPS - ASTUCES - TIPPS
- Care should be taken to make sure that the finishes are exquisite if you don't want your furniture to reach as far as the ceiling.
- Si no deseas muebles hasta el techo, cuida que sus remates sean finos.
- Si vous optez pour un meuble qui ne touche pas le plafond, soignez-en les finitions.
- Sind keine Möbel bis zur Decke gewünscht, ist darauf zu achten, dass der obere Abschluss attraktiv ist.

The oak bookshelf
fits in with the
circular-shaped
wall to create
a pleasant
all-embracing
atmosphere.

La bibliothèque
en chêne épouse
la forme circulaire
du mur et fait de
cette pièce un
endroit agréable et
confortable.

El librero de roble
se acopla a la
forma circular del
muro y crea una
grata atmósfera
envolvente.

Das Regal aus
Eiche schmiegt
sich an die
runde Wand
an und schafft
eine angenehme
Atmosphäre.

TIPS · ASTUCES · TIPPS

• *If you intend to surround a work of art by a large number of objects, then it needs to have a lot of presence.*

• *Selecciona una pieza de arte con fuerza si la vas a rodear de muchos objetos.*

• *Choisissez une œuvre d'art qui a de la personnalité si vous souhaitez l'entourer avec beaucoup d'objets.*

• *Wähle ein Kunstwerk mit grosser Ausdruckskraft, wenn es von vielen Objekten umgeben ist.*

CELLARS

CAVAS

CAVES À VINS

WEINSCHRÄNKE

Cellars are storerooms for wine. Their role in the house is unique, which means they must be located in a place that is protected from excessive sunlight, offers stable conditions and enjoys restricted access. They are also known as "cantinas" and, by extension and in everyday parlance, as bars. A cellar is a small place, ideal for get-togethers with relatives and close friends. A number of factors come into play in its design but the aim is usually to create a warm, laidback and comfortable atmosphere.

One way to bring the best out of a cellar is to build it with fine woods, glass, plates made of metal or stone, such marble or onyx, or with vegetable fibers, leather or plastic. The finishing touch can be provided by seating upholstered with materials that blend in well with the setting.

It also needs to include racks to allow certain wines to be stored in a horizontal position so that the liquid is in constant contact with the cork and to prevent direct exposure to light. Setting aside sufficient space for glassware is another factor to be borne in mind.

La cava es una bodega donde se guardan los vinos; ocupa un sitio especial en la casa y su ubicación debe tomar en cuenta condiciones que eviten la exposición excesiva a la luz solar, un clima con pocas variaciones y un acceso restringido. Se le conoce también como cantina y, por extensión y coloquialmente, como bar. Es un sitio pequeño, propicio para la convivencia familiar y con los amigos más cercanos y en su diseño pueden intervenir muchos elementos, pero generalmente su concepto tiende a crear una atmósfera amable, relajada y muy confortable.

Para hacerlo más atractivo se utilizan en su construcción maderas finas, cristal, planchas metálicas o pétreas como los mármoles, el ónix u otros como fibras vegetales, piel cuero o plásticos, y se complementa con sillas altas terminadas en materiales que armonicen con el conjunto.

El diseño debe contar con anaqueles para que cierto tipo de vinos pueda guardarse de costado a fin de mantener contacto con el corcho y que no se expongan directamente a la luz. Del mismo modo, debe calcular suficiente capacidad para la cristalería.

La cave de vin est une pièce où l'on garde, bien évidemment, le vin mais aussi les alcools. Son emplacement est minutieusement choisi dans la maison car on doit prendre en compte des facteurs comme l'exposition à la lumière, les changements de température ou les dimensions de l'entrée. On lui donne familièrement parfois le nom de buvette, de bar. L'endroit est généralement petit et il fait bon s'y réunir avec sa famille ou ses amis les plus proches. De nombreux éléments entrent en ligne de compte lorsqu'on le crée mais ce doit être avant tout un espace agréable, calme et très confortable.

Pour faire de la réserve un endroit attrayant, on utilise pour sa construction des matériaux comme des bois fins ou du verre, des plaques de métal ou de pierre (marbre, onyx) ou encore des fibres naturelles tressées, du cuir, du plastique et on la complète avec des sièges comportant des finitions recherchées et des matériaux qui s'harmonisent avec l'ensemble.

On ne doit pas oublier des étagères spéciales pour y coucher certaines bouteilles de vin afin qu'il y ait contact entre la boisson et le bouchon et pour ne pas qu'elles soient exposées à la lumière. Il ne faut pas oublier non plus l'emplacement pour la verrerie.

.

Ein Weinschrank dient der Aufbewahrung von Weinflaschen. Er nimmt im Haus einen speziellen Platz ein und bei der Festlegung des Standortes ist zu beachten, dass der Bereich nicht zu sehr dem Sonnenlicht ausgesetzt ist. Ferner wird ein gleichbleibendes Klima und ein kontrollierter Zugriff benotigt. Umgangssprachlich wird dieser Bereich oft als Bar bezeichnet. Es handelt sich um einen kleinen Bereich, der dem Zusammensein mit der Familie und engen Freunden dient. Das Design kann durch viele Elemente beeinflusst sein, aber im Allgemeinen ist es darauf ausgerichtet, eine freundliche, entspannte und sehr bequeme Atmosphäre zu schaffen.

Um das Design noch attraktiver zu gestalten, werden edle Hölzer, Glas, Metallplatten oder Steinelemente, wie Marmor, Onyx oder andere Materialien verwendet, wie zum Beispiel Naturfasern, Leder oder Plastik. Dies wird dann durch Hochstühle ergänzt, die mit der Gesamtheit harmonieren. Das Design muss Regalbretter vorsehen, damit einige Weintypen liegend gelagert werden können, damit der Wein Kontakt mit dem Korken hat; ferner ist direktes Licht zu vermeiden. Gleichermassen ist eine ausreichende Menge an Gläsern vorzusehen.

An exquisite sheet of marble covers the wooden shelves that house the glassware, while a cellar crowned by amber-colored glass is an excellent option for keeping wines and spirits.

Una sinuosa plancha de mármol cubre la estantería de madera donde se guarda la cristalería, mientras una cava con cubierta de cristal ambarino preserva cuidadosamente los vinos y licores.

Un revêtement incurvé en marbre recouvre le bar en bois dans lequel on range les verres alors que les vins et les alcools de la réserve sont bien protégés par des portes vert ambré.

Eine gewundene Marmorplatte bedeckt das Holzregal, in dem die Gläser aufbewahrt werden, während ein Weinregal mit bernsteinfarbenem Glas die Weine und Liköre schützt.

TIPS - ASTUCES - TIPPS
- *Commercial cellars save space and work very well.*
- *Las cavas comerciales ayudan a ahorrar espacio y funcionan muy bien.*
- *Les caves électriques permettent une économie d'espace et fonctionnent parfaitement.*
- *Die konventionellen Weinschränke helfen dabei, Platz zu sparen und funktionieren einwandfrei.*

The generous size of this piece of furniture affords a sense of spaciousness and elegance.

Lás cómodas dimensiones del mueble dan la sensación de amplitud al mismo tiempo que transmiten un toque de elegancia a todo el espacio.

Les dimensions généreuses du bar agrandissent l'espace tout en le rendant plus élégant.

Die bequemen Ausmasse des Möbels erwecken den Eindruck von Grossräumigkeit und gleichzeitig verleihen sie auch dem gesamten Raum einen eleganten Touch.

TIPS - ASTUCES - TIPPS

• Yellow light will lend warmth to the sleek lines of a contemporary bar.

• Dale calidez a un bar de líneas contemporáneas utilizando luz amarilla.

• Faites de votre bar aux lignes contemporaines un meuble de qualité en l'éclairant avec une lumière qui porte vers le jaune.

• Einer Bar mit modernen Linien kann durch die Verwendung von gelbem Licht Wärme verliehen werden.

The bar's light cabinet with its onyx finish is a good way to break up the textural uniformity of the floor and walls.

La caja de luz de la cantina, terminada en ónix, abre una pausa en la uniformidad de las texturas del piso y los muros.

Le comptoir en onyx sert à illuminer l'espace et rompt avec l'homogénéité formée par la texture des murs et du sol.

Die Bar aus beleuchtetem Onyx schafft eine Abwechslung in dem Raum mit einheitlichen Texturen an Böden und Wänden.

TIPS - ASTUCES - TIPPS
- *Give the bar a magical twist by turning it into a light source.*
- *Haz mágica la barra de bar haciéndola funcionar como lámpara de luz.*
- *Transformez le comptoir de votre bar en meuble magique en l'utilisant aussi comme matériel d'éclairage.*
- *Die Theke der Bar sieht magisch aus, wenn sie auch als lichtspendende Lampe funktioniert.*

A floor to ceiling wooden rack slotted into a small space stores wines and displays the bottles' labels.

Una estantería de madera, de piso a techo en un espacio reducido, almacena y deja visibles las etiquetas del vino.

Des étagères en bois qui vont du sol au plafond pour conserver les vins et mettre en évidence leur étiquette.

Ein Regal aus Holz vom Boden bis zur Decke in einem nicht allzu grossen Raum, dient der Weinlagerung, wobei die Etiketten sichtbar bleiben.

TIPS - ASTUCES - TIPPS
- A cozy corner for wine-tasting will be a big hit among wine enthusiasts.
- Un acogedor rincón para cata será el sitio predilecto de un enólogo.
- Un coin confortable pour la dégustation des vins deviendra l'endroit préféré d'un œnologue.
- Eine gemütliche Ecke für die Weinprobe, wird der bevorzugte Ort eines Weinfachmannes sein.

TIPS - ASTUCES - TIPPS
- Make sure the temperature, light and dampness are properly regulated in the cellar.
- Cuida que la temperatura, la luz y la humedad estén controladas en la cava.
- Faites en sorte que la température, la lumière et l'humidité soient toujours sous contrôle dans la cave.
- Achte darauf, dass die Temperatur, das Licht und die Feuchtigkeit im Weinkeller gleichbleibend sind.

This floor to ceiling rack is ideal for storing wine.

El diseño del mueble, con su gran altura, permite almacenar convenientemente los vinos.

Le design particulier du meuble, qui va du sol au plafond, permet de ranger aisément les vins.

Das Design des Möbels, das vom Boden bis zur Decken reicht, ermöglicht die geeignete Lagerung der Weine.

The classic cellar
in the basement
of the house with
untreated stone,
wooden beams
and oak racks.

Une cave
traditionnelle dans le
fond de la maison,
avec ses pierres
naturelles, ses poutres
de bois et ses
étagères en chêne.

La cava tradicional
al fondo de la
casa, con piedras
al natural, vigas
de madera y
estantería de roble.

Das traditionelle
Weinregal im
hinteren Bereich
des Hauses mit
Natursteinen,
Holzbalken und
Regalen aus Eiche.

TIPS - ASTUCES - TIPPS
- *Indirect lighting makes for a cozy setting in a cellar.*
- *La iluminación indirecta evoca un ambiente acogedor en una cava.*
- *L'éclairage indirect fait de la cave un endroit confortable.*
- *Indirekte Beleuchtung verleiht dem Weinkeller eine gemütliche Atmosphäre.*

The panels are distributed in a way that makes it easy to store wine and select the best bottle for the occasion.

La disposición de los entrepaños facilita el guardado de las botellas y la identificación del vino que se desea consumir.

La disposition des panneaux de bois facilite le rangement des bouteilles et l'identification des vins que l'on souhaite déguster.

Die Anordnung der Regalbretter erleichtert das Aufbewahren der Flaschen, sowie die Identifizierung des Weines, den man konsumieren möchte.

TIPS - ASTUCES - TIPPS
• You can bring out the modern feel of a cellar by combining the wooden tones of pure-lined furniture.
• Combinar los tonos de la madera en muebles de líneas puras te permitirá sentir el espacio contemporáneo.
• Associer différents tons de bois pour des meubles aux lignes pures vous permettra d'apprécier cet espace contemporain à sa juste valeur.
• Eine Kombination von verschiendenen Holztönen an Möbeln mit klaren Linien, verleiht dem Bereich einen modernen Touch.

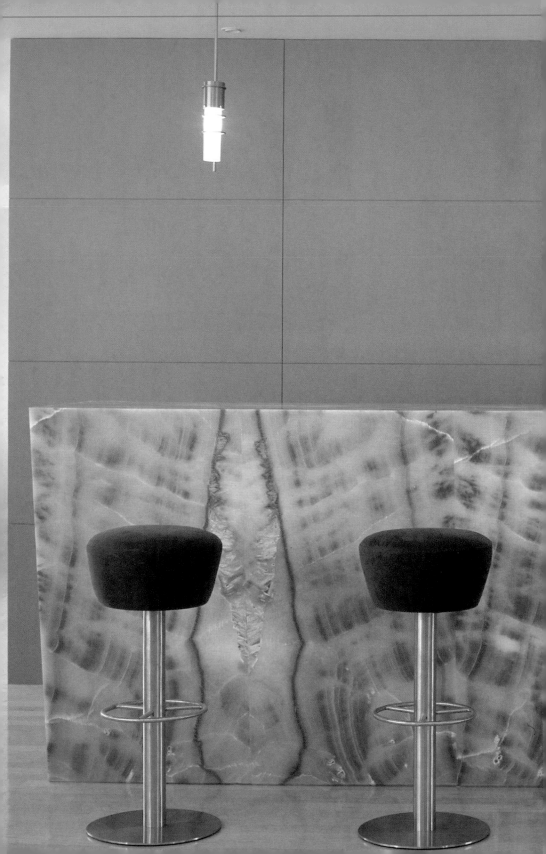

TIPS · ASTUCES · TIPPS
- Turn the appeal of natural stone patterns and designs into the centerpiece of the room.
- Aprovecha los dibujos de la piedra natural para que resalten en un ambiente.
- Profitez des veines de la pierre naturelle pour qu'elles ressortent dans la pièce.
- Nutze die Maserung des Natursteins, um im Raum einen besonderen Blickfang zu schaffen.

These drawers, in
the form of niches,
display the bottles
head-on.

En las gavetas,
en forma de nicho,
se exhiben las
botellas de frente.

Dans les casiers en
forme de niches,
les bouteilles
reposent couchées.

In den Schubfächern
in Nischenform
werden die Flaschen
nach vorne gerichtet
aufbewahrt.

The bar, with its fine wooden shelves, boasts the same textures and harmony as the main room.

El bar, con su estantería de maderas finas, comparte las texturas y la armonía de la sala principal.

Le bar, avec son bois fin, s'harmonise avec les textures utilisées pour cette pièce.

Die Bar mit Regalen aus Edelholz weist die gleiche Textur und Harmonie wie das Wohnzimmer auf.

TIPS - ASTUCES - TIPPS
- *The grain of wood can be used to create a wall brimming with artistic richness.*
- *Si juegas con el veteado de la madera podrías generar un muro artístico.*
- *Si vous parvenez à jouer sur les veines du bois, votre mur relèvera de l'œuvre d'art.*
- *Durch Spielen mit der Maserung des Holzes, kann eine künstlerische Wand geschaffen werden.*

FURNITURE
MUEBLES
MEUBLES
MÖBEL

Options for storage that can be used in any part of the house include additional items of furniture with shelves, either open or with doors, for storing all types of articles, such as tablecloths, crockery and cutlery, and displaying items of interest to the family, like souvenirs, decorations, works of art, paintings and photos, among other things. Drawers can be used for keeping original documents.

The design should preferably be original, but a commonly-used alternative is the reconditioning of old items of furniture obtained from a bazaar or inherited, which afford an undecipherable sense of warmth. This furniture also performs a decorative role and will provide any room with an atmosphere that reflects the nature of the house's occupants or their activities.

Comfort and practicality are key factors in the design, along with tastefulness and creativity, for transforming a given space into something that makes a valuable esthetic contribution to the room, because of its shape, the materials it is made from and the objects it displays.

Entre otras ideas para guardar se halla la disposición de muebles adicionales con repisas, anaqueles y puertas donde es posible almacenar todo tipo de enseres, como manteles, vajillas, cubiertos y demás objetos, independientemente de que son muy útiles para colocar adornos, obras de arte, pinturas, entre otras. El mueble es, de preferencia, original, pero muchos interioristas recurren a incorporar muebles antiguos, piezas recuperadas de algún bazar o de alguna herencia familiar.

Su función es, igualmente, decorativa y su presencia en cualquier habitación proporciona una atmósfera que define la personalidad o las aficiones de los habitantes de la casa.

En su concepto imperan la comodidad y la funcionalidad, pero también el buen gusto y la creatividad para convertir un espacio en un rincón de gran valor estético, tanto por su forma, por los materiales en que está trabajado, como por los objetos que se exhiben en él.

Les étagères, ouvertes ou fermées avec des portes, sont une des idées possibles pour ranger du linge de table, de la vaisselle, des couverts. On peut placer ces étagères partout dans la maison et on peut les utiliser aussi pour y installer des souvenirs, des décorations, des œuvres d'art, des peintures, des photographies ... Qui plus est, les tiroirs peuvent être utiles pour y ranger des documents de première main.

Leur design doit être, en général, original mais on réutilise souvent des vieux meubles, des pièces récupérées dans une quelconque brocante ou qui nous viennent d'un héritage familial pour donner de l'authenticité à la pièce où elles se trouveront. Leur fonction est également décorative et leur présence est un reflet de la personnalité et des goûts des propriétaires. On a tendance à rechercher d'abord la commodité et l'aspect pratique, mais cela n'exclut pas le bon goût et la créativité afin de doter la pièce d'une grande valeur esthétique, tant en ce qui concerne leur forme que les matériaux utilisés pour leur construction ou les objets qu'ils accueillent.

In Bezug auf die Unterbringung von Gegenständen und in jedem Bereich des Hauses werden zusätzliche Möbel mit Regalbrettern benötigt, die offen oder geschlossen sein können und in denen alle Art von Utensilien untergebracht werden können, wie Tischdecken, Geschirr und Besteck. Ferner sind so die Gegenstände sichtbar, die von familiärem Interessen sind, wie Andenken, Dekoration, Kunstwerke, Gemälde, Fotos usw. In den Schubladen werden vor allem Dokumente untergebracht.

Das Design sollte vorzugsweise originell sein und in einigen Fällen wird darauf zurückgegriffen, antike Möbel wieder herzurichten; Stücke, die auf einem Basar erworben wurden oder aus dem Familienerbe stammen und der Atmosphäre einen Touch von Wärme verleihen. Die Funktion ist ebenfalls dekorativ und die Präsenz im Zimmer führt zu einer Atmtosphäre, die Aufschluss über die Persönlichkeit oder Vorlieben der Hausbewohner gibt. Das Konzept ist hauptsächlich durch die Bequemlichkeit und Funktionalität geprägt, aber gleichzeitig auch durch guten Geschmack und Kreativität, damit der Raum in einen Bereich mit grossem ästhetischem Wert verwandelt wird, und dies sowohl aufgrund der Form, der Materialien, die Verwendung finden und der Gegenstände, die dort zu sehen sind.

There is a stylish simplicity about the way this piece of furniture houses the TV and related artifacts. Its two half shelves display ornamental objects.

El mueble guarda, con elegante sencillez, el equipo de video y todo lo relacionado con él. En sus dos medios entrepaños exhibe objetos de decoración.

Ce meuble simple et élégant accueille l'équipement audio et vidéo. Sur les deux demi étagères, on peut admirer des objets décoratifs.

Das Möbel dient mit einfacher Eleganz der Aufbewahrung der Videoausrüstung und allen dazugehörigen Accessoires. Auf den beiden halben Regalbrettern befinden sich Dekorationsgegenstände.

TIPS - ASTUCES - TIPPS
- *Groups of objects are a good way to achieve a sense of balance.*
- *Colocar series de objetos agrupadas siempre conllevará a un equilibrio.*
- *Placer des séries d'objets identiques apporte un certain équilibre.*
- *Das Anbringen einer Serie von Objekten in Grüppchen, führt immer zu einem Gleichgewicht.*

A large wardrobe offering two perspectives and a dual role divides different areas of the house.

Un gran armario con dos vistas y doble función, separa los ambientes de la casa.

Un grand meuble avec une ouverture offrant deux façades et deux fonctions, sépare un côté de la pièce de l'autre.

Ein grosser Schrank mit zwei Fronten und doppelter Funktion trennt zwei Bereiche des Hauses.

TIPS - ASTUCES - TIPPS
- *Experiment with cubes and squares to create a well-balanced set of drawers embedded in the wall.*
- *Juega con cubos y cuadrados y genera una armónica cajonera empotrada en la pared.*
- *Jouez avec les cubes et les carrés et vous obtiendrez un ensemble harmonieux d'étagères encastrées dans le mur.*
- *Kissen sind Elemente, die mit einer bestimmten Freizügigkeit in die Dekoration integriert werden können.*

This item of furniture performs its role as the foundation of the room's decorative style with aplomb. Its design, based on perfect cubes, is very much in synch with the furniture and frames the fireplace.

El propósito del mueble es ser la base de la decoración del ambiente. El diseño, de cubos perfectos, armoniza con el mobiliario y enmarca el hogar de la chimenea.

La base décorative de cette pièce est constituée par les étagères, faites à partir de cubes réguliers, qui se fondent dans le mobilier tout en encadrant la cheminée.

Der Zweck des Möbels ist es, die Grundlage der Dekoration des Bereiches zu bilden. Das Design mit perfekten Vierecken harmoniert mit den Möbeln und rahmt den offenen Kamin ein.

TIPS - ASTUCES - TIPPS
• White shelves on a white wall will make your living room look neat and orderly.
• Un mueble repisero blanco sobre un muro blanco dará sensación de pulcritud y orden a tu sala de TV.
• Des étagères blanches sur un mur de la même couleur feront du salon télé un endroit propre et bien ordonné.
• Möbel mit abwechslungsreichen Formen verleihen dem Raum Dynamik.

These four boxes have been symmetrically embedded into the wall as a harmonious complement for the console on which the TV and other family entertainment equipment sit.

Los módulos, empotrados simétricamente en el muro, se complementan armónicamente con la consola que soporta el equipo de video y todo lo relacionado con el entretenimiento familiar.

Les éléments fixés symétriquement sur le mur s'associent harmonieusement avec la console où l'on trouve l'ensemble vidéo et tout ce qui a rapport avec la détente en famille.

Die Module, die symmetrisch in die Wand eingelassen wurden, kombinieren auf harmonische Weise mit der Konsole, auf der sich die Videoausrüstung sowie weitere Unterhaltungselemente befindet.

TIPS - ASTUCES - TIPPS
• Why not include an item of white furniture to really highlight the ambience?
• Intenta incluir un mueble blanco puro para realzar el ambiente.
• Essayer de placer un meuble blanc afin d'embellir l'atmosphère de la pièce.
• Versuche doch einmal, ein rein weisses Möbelstück zu verwenden, um die Atmosphäre hervorzuheben.

Wooden items, including a large closed wardrobe and drawers, conspire with the leather-upholstered furniture and, once again, dark wood to create a welcoming atmosphere.

Las piezas de madera, entre ellas el gran armario cerrado, y los cajones, crean una atmósfera envolvente en la estancia con muebles de piel.

Les éléments en bois, comme les grands placards fermés et les tiroirs de la table basse, donnent à ce salon tout en cuir une atmosphère confortable.

Die Möbelstücke aus dunklem Holz, wie der grosse geschlossene Schrank, der Plafond und die Gittertrennwand, schaffen eine gemütliche Atmosphäre im Bereich der Regale und der Ledermöbel.

TIPS - ASTUCES - TIPPS
- *A sliding door will provide an area with spatial flexibility.*
- *Utiliza una puerta corrediza como cerramiento y lograrás flexibilidad espacial.*
- *Utilisez comme séparation une porte coulissante afin de faire de l'espace un endroit multifonctionnel.*
- *Verwende eine Schiebetür zum Abtrennen des Raumes, so bleibt der Bereich flexibel.*

architectonic   arquitectónicos   architectoniques   architektonische

photographic   fotográficos   photographiques   fotografische